SOME DEEPER SEC
HUMAN DEVELOPMENT

IN THE

LIGHT OF THE GOSPEL OF ST. MATTHEW

A Course of three Lectures given on
1st, 9th, and 23rd November, 1909, in Berlin

BY

RUDOLF STEINER

(From a Shorthand Report unrevised by the Lecturer,)

1935
LONDON
RUDOLF STEINER PUBLISHING CO.
54 Bloomsbury Street, W.C.1. and

ANTHROPOSOPHIC PRESS
NEW YORK CITY

PRELIMINARY REMARKS

From "The Story of My Life," by
Rudolf Steiner

THE FOLLOWING PASSAGE from "The Story of my Life," by Rudolf Steiner, may well serve as an introduction to the publication of this spoken lecture which first appeared privately at the express wish of the members of the Anthroposophical Society, and now is given out publicly in book form :—

" Two results had now come from my anthroposophic work: first, my books published to the world, and, secondly, a great number of lectures which were at first to be considered as privately printed and to be sold only to members of the Theosophical (later the Anthroposophical) Society. These were really reports on the lectures, more or less well done, and which I, for lack of time, could not correct. It would have pleased me best if spoken words had remained spoken words. But the members wished the printed copies. So this came about. If I had then had time to correct the reports, the restriction, ' for members only ' would not have been necessary. For more than a year now this restriction has been allowed to lapse.

"At this point in my life story it is necessary to explain, first of all, how the two things—my published books and this privately printed matter—combine to form that which I have elaborated as anthroposophy.

"Whoever wishes to trace my inner struggle and labour to set anthroposophy before the consciousness of the present age must do this on the basis of the writings published for general circulation.

"In these I explained myself in connection with all that is present in the striving of this age for knowledge. Here was given what took form for me more and more in ' spiritual perception ' and became the structure of anthroposophy—in a form that is certainly incomplete, from many points of view.

"Together with this purpose of building up anthroposophy and thereby serving only that which results when one has information from the world of spirit to give to the modern world of culture, there now appeared the other demand—to face fully whatever was manifested in the members as the need of their souls, their longing for the spirit.

"Most of all there was a strong inclination to hear the Gospels and the Biblical writings generally, set forth in that which had evolved as the anthroposophic light. Persons wished to attend courses of lectures on these revelations given to mankind.

" While private courses of lectures were held in the sense then demanded, something else arose in consequence. Members only attended these courses. These were acquainted with the elementary information coming from anthroposophy. It was possible to speak to them as to persons advanced in the realm of anthroposophy. The manner of these private lectures was such as could not appear in writings intended wholly for the public.

" In private groups I dared to speak about things in a manner which I should have been obliged to shape quite differently for a public presentation if these matters had been designed from the first for such an audience.

" Thus in both of these—the public and the private writings—there was really something derived from two different bases. All the *public* writings are the result of what struggled and laboured within me; in the privately printed matter, the Society itself shares in this struggle and labour. I hear of the strivings in the soul-life of members, and through my vital living-within what I thus hear, the nature of the course is determined."

Because of these labours arising from the reality of the soul-needs of members, this privately printed matter *must* be judged differently from that published outwardly from the first. The contents of these were intended to be communicated by word of mouth, not by print; what was spoken on these occasions was the result of close observation in the course of time, of the soul-needs of members.

What is found in the published writings is suited to the demands of Anthroposophy as such; the way in which the privately printed matter was unfolded was in accordance with the configuration of soul, of the Society as a whole.

SOME DEEPER SECRETS OF HUMAN DEVELOPMENT IN THE LIGHT OF THE GOSPEL OF ST. MATTHEW

LECTURE I.

THE LECTURES WHICH HAVE BEEN GIVEN in connection with the Gospels of John and of Luke and the type of thought by which we sought to understand them, can only be described when we say that these studies arose from the following point of view: " The Being we describe as the Christ-Jesus Being—in so far as it is possible for our human understanding to describe Him at the present time—is so great, so infinite and mighty, that no consideration can result from such a study as enables us to say in any one-sided way *Who* Christ Jesus was, and what His Being signifies to each individual human soul and spirit." This would seem like disrespect towards the greatest word-problem in existence. Reverence and awe are the words which describe the attitude of mind from which our whole considerations have arisen, reverence and veneration revealed in the attitude of soul that says: try not to place human comprehension too high when approaching the greatest of problems. Try never to place too high what an ever so exalted spiritual science imparts to you, even when it rises to the highest realms, as is the case when we approach the greatest problems of life, and do not imagine that human language can possibly reach to expressing more than *one* side at best of this mighty problem.

All the lectures that have been given in the course of the last three years had as their central point one saying which we find in the Gospel of John. It is: "I am the Light of the World." All the lectures on the Gospel of John were held for the purpose of making this saying comprehensible. And other lectures given in connection with those of the Gospel of John, were for the purpose, when people had made them their own, of gradually making these words comprehensible, or at least of giving some idea of what the saying: "I am the Light of the World," means.

When you see a light shining, have you understood, just because you have seen it, that what shines there is a light? And when you have comprehended something concerning the colours and peculiarities of this light . . . . have you understood *what* it is that gives light? Do you know the sun because you can look up to the sunlight, and receive the white sunlight as a manifestation? Can you not imagine that there is something more in comprehending that which sends forth the light than the perception of the light in the brightness?

Because the Being of Whom we have been speaking said of Himself: "I am the *Light* of the World" do we necessarily understand this saying, and have we understood anything more of this Being than the revelation of Himself given in these words? All that has been given out in connection with our studies on the Gospel of John was necessary to show that the Being Who contains within Him universal wisdom *is* the Light of the World. But this Being is far more than could be described in the Gospel of John. Anyone who thinks he could grasp or understand Christ Jesus from reading the lectures on this Gospel would believe also, that from a single statement of which he barely divined the meaning, he could understand that whole luminous Being.

Following the lectures on the Gospel of John came those on the Gospel of Luke, and in these another view is presented to you. If all that has been said in our studies on the Gospel of John were taken as a means for understanding more or less the saying: "I am the Light of the world," then what was said concerning the Gospel of Luke, if understood deeply enough, can be apprehended as a transcription of the sayings: "Father, forgive them for they know not what they do," or "Father, into Thy hands I commit my Spirit." What Christ Jesus *is*—not merely as Light of the world, but as the Being Who made the greatest sacrifice of self— the Being Who united everything within Himself, yet did not lose Himself—He Who comprised within Himself the possibility of the greatest self-surrender, and is therefore the fountain-head of all compassion and love, Who pours Himself with warmth into all future human and earthly life: all this is comprised in these words and presents a *second* aspect of what we call the Being of Christ Jesus.

We have described this Being as One Who, in His compassion, realised the greatest sacrifice, and Who, through the power of His light, illumined all human existence. We have described light and love as they were in Christ Jesus, and those who understand fully and completely the lectures on the Gospels of John and Luke can divine something of what the "light" and the "love and compassion" of Christ Jesus were. We have tried to understand two qualities in Christ Jesus in their universal meaning.

What has been said concerning the Christ as the spiritual Light of the world, which as primordial wisdom, is poured into all things so that it may live and move in them, is revealed to spiritual observation and comes forth to meet us from the Gospel of John; there is no wisdom attainable by man which is not contained in some way in this Gospel. All the Wisdom of the world is there; because those who perceive the wisdom of the world in Christ Jesus, perceive it not only as it was realised in a primeval past, but as it will be realised also in a far distant future. Therefore in our studies connected with this Gospel we rise high as an eagle in the air, above all human existence. When one has developed the great ideas made possible through an understanding of the Gospel of John, one floats with these far-reaching, all-comprising ideas far above those which occur in the individual human soul. The all-comprising *world-ideas* with which this Sophia is concerned, flow into us when we occupy ourselves with the study of the Gospel of John. Then what comes to us from this Gospel appears to us to circle high as the eagle over all the occurrences of daily, hourly, momentary human fate. When we descend to observe a single human life from hour to hour, from day to day, from year to year, from century to century, from thousand year to thousand year, when we specially observe in it those forces which we call human love, one sees this love surging and welling up in human hearts and souls. One sees how, on the one hand, it gives rise in mankind to the noblest acts of heroism, and how the greatest acts of human sacrifice have resulted from love to this or that being, to this or that cause.

One sees how love produces the noblest feelings in the hearts of men, but how at the same time it is somewhat like a two-edged sword. We have, for example, a mother who deeply loves her child; the child commits some indiscretion, she loves the child so much that she cannot bring herself in her deep love to punish it. The child commits a second fault, again the mother has not the heart to punish it; and so it goes on, the child develops, becomes good for nothing, a mischief-maker in life. When speaking of things of such great moment it is as well not to take examples from the present time, so I will make use of one far removed from to-day. In the first half of the nineteenth century there was a mother who loved her child very deeply. (It must be clearly stated that such love cannot be too highly valued; it is always something appertaining to the highest attributes of mankind.) This mother loved her child, and had not the heart to punish it because of a small theft which occurred in the family; there was a second theft; again the mother could not bring herself to punish it. The child became a notorious poisoner. The child became so through the misguided and unwise love of the mother. Love can accomplish the noblest deeds when filled with wisdom. The great significance of that love which streamed into the world from Golgotha is that it was united in one Being with the Light of the world, with Wisdom. Hence when we keep these two attributes in mind our view of Christ is such that we recognise love to be the most exalted thing in the world, but we also recognise that Love and Wisdom belong in the deepest sense to one another.

What have we understood when all these different considerations concerning the Gospels of John and of Luke have been placed before us? Nothing else than those qualities in Christ Jesus which one can call the universal Light of Wisdom, and the universal Warmth of Love, which are combined in Him as in no other Being in the world, and which are beyond the reach of any human powers of understanding. While one speaks in connection with the Gospel of John of great ideas, which rise high as the flight of the eagle above the heads of men, one finds in the Gospel of Luke that which speaks at every moment to each separate human heart.

The thing of greatest significance in the Gospel of Luke is, that it fills us with a warmth which is the outward expression of love; with comprehension of that love which is ready for the greatest sacrifice, ready to give itself up, and desires nothing else than self-sacrifice.

If an example is wanted for this condition or attitude of soul that comes with the study of the Gospel of Luke, one has the feeling that it resembles in some way what is met with in the Myths of Mythras when the sacrificial animal is hurried to the place of sacrifice. A man is seated on the bull, above is seen the course of great cosmic events, below the course of earthly events. The man thrusts his knife into the body of the bleeding animal, which surrenders its life in order than man may overcome that which he must overcome. When we contemplate this sacrificial animal, found everywhere, the animal which has to be sacrificed in order that man can pursue his path of life, we experience that feeling and attitude of soul which provides the right background of emotion that should be ours when we study the Gospel of Luke. What, through all the ages, the sacrificial bull has been to those who understood what lay behind it, is summed up in this expression of love which has to be intensified in men if they are to understand something of the qualities of the love represented here. This is what we have endeavoured to impart in our study of the Gospel of Luke. Here nothing less than a second attribute of Christ Jesus is described.

But does he who knows the attributes of a Being know the whole Being? It is because in this Being we are faced with the profoundest mystery (Rätsel), the working out in us of an understanding of these two qualities is necessary, but no one should deem himself capable of comprehending this Being merely through the consideration of *two* of His qualities.

We have here described two attributes of Christ Jesus, and have neglected nothing that might help us to divine in some measure their great importance. But our veneration and respect for this Being is such that we might perhaps think we had also guessed something of other qualities hidden in Him. Suppose that yet a third quality were possible, but as this is connected with something which has not yet been given out in the courses of study within our movement, it could only be explained in a general way. It might then be said : in describing the Christ of the Gospel of John we described Him as a highly exalted Being certainly, but as a Being Who in his activities made use of the kingdom of the wisdom-filled Cherubim. He is therefore described here according to that tone or colouring called forth by the Cherubim as they float eagle-high above the earth. If He is described according to the Gospel of Luke, we tell of that which springs from the heart of Christ as the warm fire of love. We tell of what He was to the world because He worked in that exalted realm where dwells the Seraphim. The love-fire of the Seraphim streams through the universe and is communicated to our earth by Christ Jesus.

We have now to describe a third aspect of the Christ : this reveals what He became for the earth, not only because He was the Light of Wisdom, and the Warmth of Love—not only because He provided the

Cherubic and Seraphic elements in the life of the earth
—but because of what He "was" and "is" in our earthly
existence. We then consider Him as regards His
Power, as what we describe as His "working through
the kingdom of the Thrones," through whom all
strength and power comes to the world, in order that
what is comprised in the meaning of Wisdom, the meaning of Love, can attain fulfilment. The three highest
of the heavenly Hierarchies are the Cherubim, Seraphim
and Thrones. The Seraphim by their love lead us into
the depths of the human heart, the Cherubim by their
wisdom lead us up into eagle-like heights. Wisdom
streams to us from the kingdom of the Cherubim, there
devoted love becomes sacrifice, and is symbolised in the
beast of sacrifice. Strength that pulses through the
world, strength that develops power by which everything
can be realised—the creative power pulsating through
the world which has always been represented symbolic-
ally by the Lion—is that power which was brought to
our earth through Jesus Christ. This power controls
and guides all things, and when developed indicates the
extreme climax of power : this is described to us by the
writer of the Gospel of *Mark* as the third attribute of
Christ Jesus.

When, in accordance with the Gospel of John, we
speak of the great Sun-being to Whom we give the name
of Christ, we speak of the *Light* of the earthly-sun in
a spiritual sense; we also speak in this sense when, in
accordance with the Gospel of Luke, we speak of the
Warmth of Love which pours from the earthly-sun of

the Christ; and when we speak according to the Gospel
of Mark in a spiritual sense, we speak of the *Power* of
the earthly sun. Everything which exists on the earth
as power, everything which hidden or revealed operates
as force or power on earth is met with when we devote
ourselves to a study of the Gospel of Mark.

If we can venture to understand—or but faintly
divine—the ideas coming to earth as the earthly thoughts
of Christ when we rise to the contemplation of Him in
the sense of the Gospel of John; if we can feel the warm
breath of self-sacrificing love when the warmth of the
Gospel of Luke streams through our being—then, if we
can divine the Thoughts of Christ in the Gospel of John,
the Feelings of Christ in the Gospel of Luke, we learn
of the Will of Christ through the Gospel of Mark. We
then learn to know the different forces through which
Love and Wisdom can be realised.

Three attributes must have been divined by us if, to
our studies concerning the Gospels of John and Luke,
we add those we have carried out in respect of the Gospel
of Mark. We then might say: in reverence we have
drawn nigh to Thee, and have gained some faint
divination of Thy thoughts, Thy feelings, and Thy
will, and as these three attributes of Thy soul rise before
us they provide us with the noblest model of life on
earth.

* * * * * *

We have presented these studies to you as if observing a man in a quite small way, and saying: man consists of a feeling- an understanding- and a conscious-

ness-soul; we then considered the special characteristics of the feeling- the understanding- and the consciousness-soul. If we apply the expression "consciousness-soul" to the Christ, we might say : we arrive at some faint conception of what understanding is, through the Gospel of John; we acquire some comprehension of what the feeling-soul of Christ is through the Gospel of Luke; of the consciousness-soul with all its will-forces in the Gospel of Mark. This, if rightly studied, throws light on the visible and invisible nature-forces of our universe, as concentrated in the single individuality of the Christ : it throws light on the Being Who comprises within Himself all the forces of the Universe. In the Gospel of John we entered deeply into the Thoughts of this Being, and in the Gospel of Luke into His Feelings; and because as regards these one is not required to enter so profoundly into the Individuality of this Being our considerations in respect of them are *simple* compared to what we encounter in the Gospel of Mark as the "system" of all the invisible forces, both natural and spiritual, of the Universe. All this is imprinted in the Akashic Chronicle, and is reflected back to us as in a mirror when we allow this mighty document, the Gospel of Mark, to influence us. We then acquire some dim understanding of what is concentrated within the single Being of Christ—all that is otherwise distributed among the separate Beings of the Universe. We then understand, and there will appear to us in ever fuller light and splendour, all we have learnt to recognise as the elementally true and original plans of these various

Beings. When we are able to decipher all the mysteries of the Universal-Will as contained in the Gospel of Mark, we draw near with reverence to the kernel of the universe, Christ Jesus, in that we have grasped in some way His thoughts, His feeling, and His will.

In our observation of the interplay of thinking, feeling, and will, we have a picture more or less of the whole man; but we cannot fully observe thinking, feeling, and willing separately, even in an individual. If these attributes are taken together our glance even then does not reach far enough to perceive everything. While we have lightened our task considerably by separating the three soul-qualities and observing each by itself, our picture is blurred when we observe them gathered into one.

If one has studied three Gospels, those of John, Luke, and Mark, and thereby gained some perception of the thought, feeling and will of Christ Jesus, one is then able to realise what is capable of uniting these three qualities into a harmonious whole. The picture must necessarily be dim and indistinct, for no human power is fitted to gather into one individual what we have thus separated. In Being is unity, and no separateness at all; so only at the end* do we venture to assemble it into an unity. The picture has grown dim, but finally it is replaced by another, and Christ Jesus rises before us as earthly man, as man was in the beginning.

* Scilicet, in the Gospel of Matthew.—ED.

A picture of what Christ Jesus was as man, how He acted as a man in the thirty-third year of his earthly life, can be gained when we direct our studies to the Gospel of Matthew. The content of this Gospel presents us with an harmonious picture of a human being. If in the lectures on the Gospel of John we described a cosmic Divine Man Who belongs to the entire universe; if in those on the Gospel of Luke we described an outstandingly self-sacrificing Being of Love, and in those on the Gospel of Mark the World-Will acting within a single individual; then in the Gospel of Matthew we have before us the true form of the Man of Palestine, that Man Who dwelt there for thirty-three years, in Whom is united all that we have learnt to know in our studies of the three other Gospels. The form of Christ Jesus comes before us in connection with the Gospel of Matthew in a thoroughly human way, as that outstanding individual who could not, however, have been understood unless this study had been preceded by that of the other Gospels. Even if this exceptional man may then grow dim to us, yet in this weakened image we see reflected what we had gained through the other studies. We first get a picture of the *personality* of Christ through studying the Gospel of Matthew.

This is how the whole matter now comes before us, and quite differently from the way it was presented when dealing with the Gospel of John. As we have now the study of two Gospels behind us we can show in what way these two Gospels are inwardly related to each other, and how we are first able to gain a picture of

Christ Jesus when — thus fittingly prepared — we approach the *Man* Who became what He was on earth through Christ Jesus.

A divine man meets us when studying the Gospel of John; and when studying the Gospel of Luke we encounter a Being Who unites in Himself the streams, that, flowing from all sides enter into the one which developed on earth as the result of Zarathustranism and Buddhism—the teaching of compassion and love. Everything of this nature that had existed previously meets us when we direct our studies to the Gospel of Luke.

If we now turn to the consideration of the Gospel of Matthew, we are shown, in the first place, intimately and exactly, what it was that was born from out a "peculiar people," out of the ancient Hebrew race : the Man Jesus as He was rooted in His nation, the Man Jesus as He had to be within the ancient Hebrew people, and we are enabled to realise why the blood of this ancient race had to be employed in a very special way in order that it might contribute towards producing the blood of Christ Jesus for earthly humanity. In our study of the Gospel of Matthew we encounter not only the essence of the Hebraism of the past, but we learn the mission of this people for the whole world, the birth of a new age, the birth of Christianity out of the ancient Hebrew world. If through the Gospel of John we receive great, significant, and all-embracing ideas; if through the Gospel of Luke we acquire some perception of the boundless warmth of sacrificing love; if through our studies on the Gospel of Mark we gain some understanding of the forces of all the Beings and kingdoms of the universe; we now acquire a knowledge and a feeling for what dwells in humanity and in human evolution on the earth, through the life of Christ Jesus in Palestine. What Christ Jesus was as Man, what He is as Man—all the secrets of human history and human development—are contained in the Gospel of Matthew.

If the Gospel of Mark contains the secrets of the beings and kingdoms of the earth and of the cosmos appertaining to the earth, we must look for the secrets of human history to the Gospel of Matthew.

Having learnt the idea of what Sophia is through the Gospel of John, the mystery of sacrifice and love through the Gospel of Luke, having learnt of the forces of the earth and of the universe through the Gospel of Mark, we now learn of human life, human history, and human fate through the study and contemplation of the Gospel of Matthew.

If, during the seven years of our spiritual movement, we have spent four years in preparing the foundations of this teaching and three years in deepening and intensifying it, using it as a light that could be thrown on the various realms of life, there ought now to follow the study of the Gospel of Mark. Then finally, the whole structure might have been crowned through a study of Christ Jesus in reference to the Gospel of Matthew. But as human life is imperfect, this could not be, at least with all who are in the movement; it was not possible without arousing misunderstanding, to pass on to the study of the Gospel of Mark. The form of Christ would be completely misunderstood were it thought that knowledge of this Being could follow from the considerations we held on the Gospels of Luke and John; again it might be thought that everything we have ventured to say about the Gospel of Mark was applied in a one-sided way. Misunderstandings in this case might have become greater than they already were, therefore with this consideration in mind the other way had to be chosen. As careful a course of study on the Gospel of Matthew as is possible, will follow shortly. In it we will turn aside at first from the great profundities of the Gospel of Mark and thus avoid it being thought that in considering *one* attribute we have sufficiently described the whole Man; in this way we may possibly avoid misunderstandings.* In this study we shall concern ourselves first as far as possible with the coming forth of Christ Jesus from the ancient Hebrew people, and with what may be called the birth of Christianity in Palestine. On this account it is with the Gospel of Matthew that we shall concern ourselves in the following lectures, and by considering Christ Jesus as a whole, hope to avoid confusion concerning the different attributes of this Being. Then what we shall have to say later concerning the Gospel of Mark will follow more easily.

*See reference to this in the "Goetheanum," No. 44, 4th Nov., 1934.

LECTURE II.

IN THE LAST LECTURE we explained our desire to occupy ourselves with some meditations on the Gospels, and gave the reason why our present lecture would be on the Gospel of Matthew. In a certain sense the most human side of Christ Jesus is presented to us in this Gospel; on the other hand it puts before us a complete review of historical events showing how Christ Jesus evolved out of humanity itself. As we are here shown how the greatest event in earthly evolution was the result of historical evolution, we may also venture to assume that the deeper secrets concerning the rise and development of humanity are also to be found in this Gospel. I would like to take this opportunity of again emphasising the fact that the things that will be dealt with on this occasion are subtle, and that it would be very easy to do harm to the spiritual-scientific movement if the secrets dealt with here were put before the world in any one-sided way. Hence the greatest possible care should be taken with every communication concerning these things. The wish cannot be too strongly expressed that anyone desiring to present an image of the Christ should only do so if he has the patience to describe this Being from four sides as these are given to us in the Gospels.

It can be seen even in the Gospel of Luke how the

two great pre-Christian streams, that springing from
Zarathustra, and the other which reached its pre-
Christian fulfilment in Buddhism, unite, so as to pour
their combined content in the great stream of Christian
life on earth.

The Gospel of Matthew is concerned at first with a
quite different theme, namely, with showing how the
bodily nature in which the individuality of Zarathustra
incarnated evolved within the ancient Hebrew race. Its
task is to show what share the ancient Hebrew race had
in the whole evolution of mankind. It is easy to understand that when it is said that the individuality of
Zarathustra incarnated in Jesus of Bethlehem, that only
the bodily nature was born at that time out of the
Hebrew race, and that nothing else is meant than that
Zarathustra incarnated in a bodily form which had
evolved within that ancient race. If any other feeling is
introduced an entirely false picture of the truth is presented.

It becomes ever clearer to us through such considerations that an individuality such as Zarathustra had need
of the bodily nature as instrument. When an individuality descends to earth from the highest worlds, from
the divinely spiritual worlds, and incarnates in an un-
suitable bodily nature, he cannot make anything more
out of this, as instrument, than it is capable of. The
false feelings just mentioned might easily give rise to
all kinds of misunderstandings. In the Theosophical
movement it was not understood for a long time that the
bodily nature of man is the temple of the soul.

It must be remembered that we have often said : the human ego dwells in three sheaths or garments, each of which is older than the ego itself. This human ego is a being of the earth, the youngest of the human principles—the astral body had its beginning on the ancient Moon, the etheric or life-body on the ancient Sun—so that it has three stages of planetary evolution behind it; in its own way the physical body is the most completed part of man and has four planetary stages of evolution behind it. From aeon to aeon this physical body has been constructed so that it is to-day the perfect instrument within which the human ego can evolve, so that man may be able gradually to rise again to spiritual heights. Were the physical body as imperfect as the astral body and ego, human evolution would be impossible on earth.

If you understand the full significance of this you can no longer associate any false shade of feeling with the idea that Zarathustra was to be born from out of the Hebrew race. That people had to be constituted just as it was, if it were to be capable of providing a bodily nature for a being like Zarathustra. When we realise that this being had evolved to ever greater heights since the time he taught the original Persian people, we must allow it was necessary that he should be given a bodily instrument from a race commensurate to the greatness of his nature.

Throughout the evolutions of Saturn, Sun, Moon and Earth, the gods have concerned themselves with the construction of the physical body of mankind in general. We might well conclude from this that the more intimate preparation of a human body demanded much divinely-spiritual creative work before a form could be brought to the high degree of excellence that could serve Zarathustra at that time. The history of the Hebrew people had to take the course it did in order that this might come to pass. The Akashic Chronicle reveals to us, that what is found in the Old Testament agrees entirely with historical facts. Everything had to be so directed within the ancient Hebraic race that it finally reached its summit in that one personality—Jesus of Bethlehem. But special arrangements were necessary for this; it was necessary that something should be derived from the accumulated culture of the post-Atlantean age, capable of evolving those forces in man which had to be evolved, and which could replace the old faculty of clairvoyance. The Hebrew people were chosen for the purpose of providing bodies in which what we call *understanding* of the world could be organised, and this within the finest convolutions of the brain without any participation in the old clairvoyance. This was to be the mission of the Hebrew people. In Abraham, the father of the race, an individual was chosen whose body should provide a fitting instrument for this discerning thought. Everything great or important before his time had still been under the influence of ancient clairvoyance; but now a personality was to be selected who possessed a brain, not driven hither and thither by clairvoyant imaginations and intuitions, but capable of considering things purely by means of the understanding. This demanded a specially organised brain, and the person who had this brain had to be specially selected. This person we have to see in Abram or Abraham.

This accords absolutely with what is observed in the Akashic records : that the direction from which Abraham came, tended from beyond the Euphrates westward towards Canaan. Abraham was fetched, as we are told in the Bible, from Ur in Chaldea. While the echoes of ancient dim clairvoyance still remained in Egyptian civilisation as well as in that of Chaldea and Babylon, an individual was selected from the Chaldean race who relied no longer on this, but on the observations of what he beheld in the external world. With this power a civilisation was introduced, the fruits of which have permeated to this day the whole culture and civilisation of the West. This combining thought, this mathematical logic, was introduced by Abraham ; he was recognised up to the middle ages, in a certain sense, as the founder of Arithmetic. The whole trend of his thought was to consider the world in relation to *measure and number.* Such a personality was fitted to acquire a living relationship to that Divinity Who reveals Himself through the medium of the external world. All divinities, other than *Jahve,* had revealed themselves in the inwardness of men's souls ; men had to awaken Imagination, Intuition, etc., in their souls in order to know of them. In ancient India men looked up to the Sun ; they looked on the different kingdoms of the earth ; they considered what took place in the surrounding atmosphere, in the sea and so on; but all this they held to be illusion—Maya; the Indian found nothing appertaining to Divinity in these unless he attained to it through his inner Imagination, and associated this with what he beheld in the world around him. Even with regard to Zarathustra we have to realise that he could not have pointed men to the great Sun-Being if Ahura-Mazdao, the mighty Sun Being had not dawned within him. This can be seen especially with regard to the Egyptian divinities; these rose entirely from inward experiences of the soul, and were afterwards related to external things.

Everything that is connected with pre-Hebraic deities must be understood from this point of view. Jahve is that deity who was seen from *without*, who approached men from outside; who revealed Himself in wind and weather. When men penetrate to everything that exists in the world around as number, weight, and measure, they draw near to the god Jahve. In earlier times the path was entirely different. Brahma was recognised at first in the inwardness of the soul, and from there passed outwards. Jahve, on the other hand, was recognised first in the outer world, after which He could be learned of in the inwardness of a man's own soul.

This is the spiritual side of what is called the covenant of Jahve with Abraham. This man had a personality capable of understanding Jahve. The physical nature of Abraham was such that he could understand Jahve as the god who permeated and gave life to all the outer phenomena of the world.

Now because of the idiosyncracy of an individual, of Abraham, it behoves us to follow the mission of a whole people. It was necessary that Abraham's spiritual constitution should be passed on to others. This was, however, bound to the physical instrument, for everything that comes to man from outside is connected with some quite distinct organ of the physical body. The religions of ancient peoples, because founded on their shadowy clairvoyance, did not attach much weight to the way the separáte parts of the human brain were formed, but an understanding of *Jehova* was strictly bound up with this conformation. The transmission of such idiosyncracies could only take place by physical inheritance in a people closely related by blood.

Something special had therefore to happen. Abraham had to have descendants capable of carrying on the development of that special constitution of the physical body, which until then had been formed by the gods, and which attained its highest flowering in Abraham. The formation of the human body which until then had been the work of the gods, had now to be undertaken unaided and carried further by man himself, and this had to be done throughout many generations. A brain capable of comprehending Jahve had to be maintained through physical inheritance. The covenant between Jahve and Abraham had also to be passed on to his descendants. But with this there was associated an extraordinary sacrifice of the individuality of Abraham to Jahve; for man only acquires the possibility of developing any special constitution further, if this is used according to the intention with which it was created. For instance, if the hand is to attain a great aptitude for some special object, this can only be done if its powers are developed according to the intention with which it was created. If the physical qualities of the brain, as an instrument for comprehending Jahve, were to be developed, self-sacrifice on the part of Abraham, and comprehension of Jahve by him, had to reach their greatest imaginable height.

This actually took place! In the Bible we are told what happened. Sacrifice reaches its highest point when one sacrifices what one is to become in the future. Abraham was to sacrifice his son Isaac to Jahve. In doing so he would have to sacrifice the whole Hebrew people, all he was himself, and all that had been brought into the world through him. Abraham was the first man to understand Jahve. If he wished to show his complete devotion to Him, he would have to give himself up to Him entirely. Through the sacrifice of his only offspring he renounced any continuance of his race in the world; and he carried this sacrifice so far that he was prepared to sacrifice Isaac; he was willing to do this. Isaac was given back to him. What does this mean? It means something tremendous. Isaac is given back to him by Jahve himself: this means that Abraham has reached a point where the mission which had been given to him by virtue of his own individuality is not to be carried over by *him* to a later world, but he is to accept it as a gift from Jehova in the person of his own son. Anyone who thinks over this will realise that herein lies a fact of world-wide historical import, one which throws light to an infinite extent on the secrets of the historical growth and development of humanity.

Now let us consider the progress of events. Through the sacrifice made by Abraham to Jahve it was possible that what up to then had been called into existence by the gods could make further progress by itself. We know that physical man is in fact born out of the universe. We know that his corporeal nature as it is on earth is connected with number, measure and weight, with all the laws ruling in the realm of the stars. Man is born from the starry world; he bears within him the laws of that world. The laws of the starry world had to be engraven, as it were, on the blood that flowed down from Abraham through all the generations of the ancient Hebrew race. In this people everything had to be so ordered that the stream of the law (Gesetzmässigkeit) as it was ordered from out the universe might continue, that it might continue in the number, measure and weight of the human physical body. We find this repeated in a saying that has been dreadfully misrepresented in the Bible. The expression referred to does not mean that God will make the Israelites as numerous as the stars of heaven, but that in the way they continue to develop and spread over the earth the same law, the same relationship of numbers will rule, as rules in the stars in the heavens. That which the Hebrew people were to hand down, or pass on, was to be ordered in accordance with the numerical harmony of the stars (Zahlenverhältnisse).

We see how this came to pass. Isaac had two sons, Jacob and Esau. We see also how everything which flowed down in the direct line through the blood of the generations continued to evolve, while that which belonged to the Esau-stream was eliminated and removed from the true line. Jacob had twelve sons, corresponding to the twelve divisions of the Zodiac through which the sun journeys in the heavens, to maintain the order of the stars. This is the inward measure of the law (Gesetzmäsigkeit). In the life and continuity of the Hebrew people we see an exact reflection of number and measure, as these obtain in the heavens. Abraham was ready to sacrifice his son Isaac; because of this he received his whole mission back again from Jahve. Instead of Isaac a ram or lamb was sacrificed. What does this mean?

Something very profound is concealed in this. That physical human attribute which was to pass by descent through the race, to which certain faculties were attached, and on which the comprehension of measure and number in accordance with mathematical logic depended, was to continue and be received as a gift from Jahve. But in order that it might be preserved pure and unmixed, it was necessary that all dim clairvoyance should be renounced; all Imagination, Intuitions, and the inflow of all those Revelations such as were found in all religions in olden times up to those of the Chaldeans and Egyptians. Every gift from the spiritual world had to be renounced. The last of these to remain when all the earlier gifts had grown dim, was expressed by the mystic symbol of the Ram. Here the two horns of the ram referred to the sacrifice of the two-petalled Lotus flower : the last clairvoyant gift was offered up after the earlier ones had already been renounced. In order that Isaac might retain the physical quality of this organ, the last clairvoyant attribute—the gift of the Ram or two-petalled Lotus flower—had to be sacrificed.

The mission of this people continued in that the Abraham-faculty was handed down from generation to generation. The moment clairvoyance reappeared atavistically, the moment someone could again see into the spiritual world, so strong a reaction took place that the person having this gift was at once driven away; he was not suffered within the community. Antipathy to the gift of the Ram was revealed in enmity. This is seen with regard to Joseph. In his dreams he received prophetic illumination from the spiritual world. His banishment from among his own people is entirely comprehensible, because what he possessed was not in line with the mission of the Hebrew people. He was cast out by his brethren because a relic of the old clairvoyance had reappeared in him. Joseph had to go to Egypt because he had fallen away from the mission of his people. Such is the deep significance of what is here told us !

We now see how through this a personality, in whom an ancient legacy had been retained which the

Hebrew people could only look upon as something existing before the time of Abraham—through Joseph— something was brought about which was once more of great importance in the evolution of the ancient Hebrew people for the fulfilment of their mission. To the Hebrew people the door in a certain sense was closed, which led the Indian and Persian peoples to their religion by means of the old dim clairvoyance. For them the door was closed! They looked out into the world that was regulated according to measure and number, and they recognised Jahve or Jehova as the Unity by whom all these things were ordered. One thing they still knew, which was: that all this on which they looked, all they encountered in Jahve as creator of world-phenomena, was one and the same with the human ego (Ichheit). But no Imaginations, no individual inner experiences arose within this people concerning these things; hence they had to learn of them from outside. This means they had to learn of them from a people who still had these inner experiences.

It was the person of Joseph that formed the connecting link between the ancient Hebrews and the Egyptians; a people from whom the ancient Hebrews could learn what they were no longer able to experience for themselves. What a man can bring to his own consciousness when he has had *individual* inner experiences—knowledge and experience of the outer world and at the same time inner Imagination—had to meet each other. This meeting took place when the Hebrews came in touch with a people who still had clairvoyant experiences to a large extent—the Egyptian people. They had to bring such inner capacities into harmony with what they had gained through mathematical logic. But the Hebrews could only be led to the Egyptian by a personality who himself possessed something of Imagination. Joseph provided the right connecting link because he had these capacities. He was able to be of service to the Egyptians because he possessed qualities of two kinds : first, he had the ancient clairvoyance from before the time of Abraham, and he was also familiar with that which the Egyptians attained to through their clairvoyant endowment. But what the Egyptians did not possess was mathematical logic, which means that they were unable to apply what they possessed as Imagination to ordinary physical life. When anything unprecedented happened Pharaoh was unable to organise matters correctly. Imagination one might have, but—if something disturbing occurred— other capacities such as the Egyptians did not possess were required; it was necessary to think cleverly in accordance with measure and numbers and to organise the relation of these to each other. This twofold capacity Joseph possessed. On this account he was able to give good advice to the Egyptian court. He provided the right link between the Hebrews and the Egyptians. He was capable to do this because the Jehova-teaching, which until then had been a summing up of *external reality*, like a *mathematical world-picture*, received colour and content from the inner Imagination existing in Egypt.

This relationship and harmony between ancient Egyptian experiences and an understanding of cosmic relationships was brought about through Moses. Once this had been done the people could be led back so that what they had seen and heard, not experienced, in Egypt, might continue to influence them in its own way. The important thing was that the gift to Abraham should remain pure and unmixed with the blood of other peoples, that the special quality in the blood should not be contaminated, but that what this ancient people had won should be preserved for the race. So the inheritance from olden times—which in the people of Egypt was the gift of wisdom—was implanted in the ancient Hebrews by Moses along with his mathematical logical faculties. They had, however, to be torn once more from their surroundings, because the new capacities which were to be passed on to their descendants could only be passed on by a people belonging to the race of Abraham.

The life of this people continued. Because the pre-ordained conditions tended to become ever finer, because the blood of the people tended ever more towards these pre-ordained conditions and developed as it did throughout the generations, it became possible at a certain point of time for the bodily-nature of the child Jesus to develop from among them a body, into which the personality of Zarathustra was able to enter. For this purpose the Hebrew people had to grow strong and powerful.

If, in accordance with the Gospel of Matthew, we

trace their fate onwards from the time of the Judges and
Kings, we see from the circumstances in which we find
them that this people often erred; and that this was
necessary so as to bring about what had to happen.
Especially it was necessary that this people should
experience misfortune. This is shown in the leading of
them into captivity in Babylon. We shall see how this
developed their special characteristics, and how it was
necessary that they should come in contact with the
other side of the old tradition as met with in Babylon,
when they were ripe for being led back to that which
they had forsaken.

This is one point. The other is, that at the very
time when the Hebrews were brought in contact with
the Babylonians, a mighty teacher from the East was
teaching among them, and some of the best among the
Hebrews were able to come under the illuminating
influence of this great teacher. It was the time when
Zarathustra, in the form of Zaratas or Nazarathos,
taught in the regions to which the Jews had been taken.
Some of the best of the Prophets came under his influence. Here he was able to do as much as was possible
with this people, for the blood had already brought
about certain results, and then certain other influences
had to make an impression on them from outside.

One would indeed not go far wrong if one compared
this whole evolution with the evolution of a single
slowly developing human being. We have in this case
a newly-born child; it grows as regards its body until
its seventh year under the care of its parents. During

this time it is principally affected by the influences of the physical plane. Then a development begins which starts with the ether body being born in the right way; this evolution is based on the development of the memory, that which it is possible to acquire when the ether body is strengthened as it should be. In the third period that begins which is called : the entrance of man's astral body into relationship with the outer world. Here he must acquire his power of judgment. The Hebrew people travelled this road in a very special way. They passed through the first period, from the time of Abraham to the early Kings; this may be compared in a single life with the period up to the seventh year. During this time everything was done to establish the characteristic quality of the blood. All we are told of in this period : the wanderings of Abraham, the forming of the twelve tribes, the order in which the different parts of the Mosaic law were given, the perils of the desert, all these can be compared with what takes place in the first seven years of a man's life on this physical plane. Then follows the second period, that of inner consolidation, the rule of the Kings up to the time of the Babylonian captivity. Then comes the influence of the Chaldeans on Hebrew civilisation, the Oriental ʿinfluence of the teaching of the Magi, and the appearance of the great leader who, in the person of Zarathustra, poured his Oriental influence on to the Hebrew people 550 to 600 years before our era. At that time he was already actively preparing a fitting bodily nature for a later incarnation. In this way throughout the generations from Abraham onwards, those possibilities and conditions evolved more and more out of which a suitable bodily-nature could be born, into which Zarathustra could later incarnate.

The Gospel of Matthew represents this evolution in particular with wonderful fidelity, in that it allows a three-fold grouping to emerge. We have three times fourteen partitions: from Abraham to David fourteen; from David to the Babylonian captivity again fourteen; and from the Babylonian captivity to Christ Jesus again fourteen; this gives three times fourteen partitions or forty-two in all, showing how, as regards His bodily nature, Jesus was an extract of everything which from the time of Abraham downwards had been prepared through the varied vicissitudes of the ancient Hebrew people. And now a human being was to appear, who summed up in *one* man all the qualities that had been gathered together, as it were, in a sequence of generations, and Who gave expression to them in His soul, and in the activities of His soul.

The whole Hebraic evolution since Abraham was summed up in one man, and reached its climax in the Jesus of the Gospel of Matthew.

How could this come to pass? It could only be possible if the whole course of this evolution were recapitulated in the soul-life of one man. Zarathustra came approximately from the neighbourhood of Ur of the Chaldees, but spiritually he came from the Mysteries whence Abraham had come. It was there the " Golden Star " was first seen. It started there, and from thence

the Magi followed it : this star was the incarnating
Zarathustra himself, who travelled the road that
Abraham had formerly travelled, and set over the place
where the child was born. At that moment the
individuality of Zarathustra incarnated in the child
Jesus Who was born in Bethlehem. This was known
to the Magi, they followed the star, which means they
followed their great teacher Zarathustra, who was about
to incarnate.

What concerns us now is that this path
should really continue : that within the person of the *one*
Jesus the entire extract of Hebrew civilisation was
concentrated. In the first place, we see that in spirit a
sacrifice is repeated : the sacrifice of Isaac. It was repeated
in spirit in the sacrifice offered by the three Magi from
the East : Gold, Frankincense and Myrrh were offered
by them. Something is seen here which again recalls
an earlier event of the ancient Hebrew people. Everything connected with the birth of this Jesus-child is in
some way a reflection of the vicissitudes of the Hebrew
race : in it we have a Joseph who had an inheritance
of dreams, and who represented the connecting link
between the Hebrew and the Egyptian peoples; again
we find a Joseph who had dreams, and in a dream was
informed not only that Jesus would be born, but that
he should take Him to Egypt.

The progress of Zarathustra in the bodily form of
the child Jesus continues. As he had followed the path
taken by Abraham on the physical plane from Ur in
Chaldea to Canaan, so he now continued his journey to ﹏

Egypt—and the child was brought back out of Egypt,
as the Hebrew people were also led out of Egypt. Thus
at the beginning of the life of Jesus of Bethlehem, Who
was later called the Nazarene, we find a repetition of the
various vicissitudes of the ancient Hebrew people up to
their return from Egypt into the promised land of
Palestine. That which had taken place through long
centuries as the external history of the Hebrew race was
repeated in the vicissitudes of that human being who
appeared as Zarathustra in the bodily form of Jesus of
Bethlehem. This, according to the meaning of the
Gospel of Matthew, if taken in a wide sense, is the
secret of human history. Human history is not under- \
stood unless it is recognised that in the fate of great
outstanding individuals who have a special mission we
have to see a repetition of the whole of evolution
throughout the long course of centuries; that these men
have to take up into themselves in one incarnation an
extract of all that has taken place in history.

Christ Jesus had indeed to take up far more, but
in the first place His bodily nature had to be suitably
prepared, and this could only be done by the means I
have described.

At what point of time was it that this short recapitu-
lation of the whole history of the Hebrew people occurred
within the personality of Jesus?

To understand this moment we must review the
following evolutionary facts, for which during many
years I have tried to prepare your thoughts. Consider
the following : humanity arose from a primeval evolu-

tion in which everything which bound men together in
love was connected with the blood tie. Those people
loved each other who were closely connected by blood,
and only those married who were connected by such
ties. There was no other love at that time, and this is
why marriage was associated with blood relationship.
This was called "close marriage"; humanity resulted
from close marriage. These bonds were then broken
asunder more and more in various parts of the earth.
Among all kinds of peoples we can trace how it was
considered an extraordinary occurrence when the transi-
tion to "distant marriage" was introduced, when men
and women of different families married. In all myths
and legends this is described as a strange occurrence, for
instance, in the Song of Gudrun. This always made a
strange impression on people. Two tendencies have
been active in mankind during this evolution. In
the bringing of people together through the bond of the
blood, the divine Spiritual Principle has ever been active
which desired that mankind should be one. Against
this the Luciferic Principle was actively at work desiring
that each man should stand alone, that every individual
should become as powerful and great as possible. Both
principles had to be present in human nature, both
forces had to be active in human evolution.

Now these two forces were at work all through the
advancing course of human evolution : the Divine
Spiritual forces and also those Luciferic forces which
had remained behind on the Moon, forces desirous of
preventing people from losing themselves, and preferring

that they should become quite independent. These two
forces worked within human evolution; and the human
ego, which is a product of the earth, was therefore torn
hither and thither; on one side it was attracted to human
love, on the other to inner self-sufficiency. Now, at a
certain point of time, a crisis arose regarding the inter-
action of these two forces. This crisis, or turning point
in human affairs, occurred when through the action of
the Roman Empire people were very much intermingled
over a great part of the earth. It was indeed a moment
big with fate for human evolution; the moment when
the decisive question concerning close or distant
marriage had to be clearly put. People were faced with
the danger either of losing their ego through remaining
in separate family groups, or of losing all connection with humanity and becoming merely separate,
independent, egotistic individuals. This decisive
moment had come. What was to happen? Something
quite definite. The human ego had to become sufficiently
ripe to develop within itself. It had to develop that
which for the first time could be called independence
and freedom, and be able to evolve soul-love freely from
within itself—love that was no longer bound by the ties
of blood. The ego was faced with this decisive moment.
In complete freedom it had to become more fully aware
of itself. The whole of. the humanity of the ancient
world, with the exception of the Oriental peoples, was
now confronted with a new birth of the ego, with a birth
by which this ego could rise to a love born from within
itself. The ego was now to evolve love through free-

dom, and freedom through love. And in fact a being
who can do this is only then completely human. He is
first a true man who evolves such an ego. For he who
only loves because of the existence of the blood tie is
forced to love and merely expresses at a higher stage
what exists on a lower—the animal stage. At the
moment I am now describing, man reached his full
development for the first time. At this moment, an
influence was to spread over the earth which was to make
men truly men.

· Recall what I have said to you on countless occasions, that the being of man consists of three parts: of
the physical body, which he has in common with
minerals; the etheric body, which he has in common
with plants; and of the astral body in which up till then
love was really situated, and which he has in common
with animals. Through his fully evolved ego, man is
the crown of earthly creation. All other earthly beings
have names which can be given them from outside, they
are objects. The ego has a name which it can give
only to itself. In the ego the Godhead speaks, earthly
connections speak in it no more, the kingdom of the
Spirit speaks in the ego; the Spirit from Heaven speaks
when the ego has come completely to itself. One might
say that till this time there had been three kingdoms—
the mineral, vegetable and animal kingdoms; also
another kingdom that certainly had sprang from these,
but which had not yet reached perfection, had not
yet received its whole super-earthly nature into itself.
This kingdom, which consisted in the fact that into an

ego-nature (Ichheit), which till then could not be found anywhere on earth, the spiritual world, the Kingdom of Heaven, had entered; this kingdom is called in the language of the Bible "The Kingdom," or "The Kingdoms of the Heavens," or it is simply spoken of as "The Kingdom of God."

The Kingdom of Heaven is nothing else than another way of describing the "human kingdom." If we speak of a mineral, a vegetable, and animal kingdom, we can also in accordance with the Bible speak of a fourth kingdom—"The Kingdom of Heaven." Thus, according to the Bible meaning, the human kingdom is "The Kingdom of Heaven," and those who at that time could view the whole course of human evolution according to the meaning of the Mysteries, might have spoken as follows: "Look back into the ages of the past: humanity at that time was being led towards human existence, the Kingdom of Heaven had not then come to earth; but the time has now come when the Kingdom of Heaven is coming down to earth."

The forerunner of Christ said, as did also Christ Jesus Himself, "The Kingdom of Heaven is at hand." In these words the profound import of this age is revealed. In it the birth of Christ Jesus was to take place. He was to bring those powers to humanity through which the ego could develop the qualities of which I have spoken. The whole of human evolution is divided therefore into two parts. A pre-Christian part when the Kingdom of Heaven had not yet come to earth, and another when it was on earth, indicating the time when the human kingdom had reached its highest significance. The ancient Hebrew race was chosen to provide the bodily nature—the physical sheath, within which a Being, capable of becoming the bearer of this Heavenly Kingdom, could evolve.

These are the secrets that are revealed, when we consider these matters historically in the deeper sense associated with the Gospel of Matthew. So to the two streams that have been described and which we have learnt to know as those contributing towards Christianity —the streams of Zarathustranism and Buddhism—we have to add a third : the Hebraic stream, provided by this ancient people. We can now say : once upon a time there were leaders like Buddha and Zarathustra who desired to bring (to Christianity) the offering of their religious streams. For this a temple had to be raised, which temple could only be constructed by the ancient Hebrew people; it was they who constructed the temple for the bodily nature of Jesus. Both the earlier streams had a share in building this temple : for it Zarathustra first offered sacrifice by incorporating in this body : for it Buddha later offered a sacrifice by permitting his Nirmanakaya to pass into the other Jesus. Thus these two streams were united.

In order that I might convey to you what, in a certain sense, are hidden thoughts, I have presented you to-day with but an abstract, fleeting sketch of these deep Mysteries. But so that I might for once give out such hidden thoughts, they had to be described, for the most part, in an abstract way. Later on this will be carried further, so that you may form a picture of the mission of the ancient Hebrew people, and of the unique way in which Christ Jesus evolved from it. The strange fact is revealed how from history, from out the ordinary course of evolution, a Being of infinite importance, of everlasting worth, emerged, of a worth that can endure for ever. Thus it is gradually revealed how out of a perishable world something can evolve which will endure for all eternity.

LECTURE III.

I N THE LAST LECTURE we had something to say in connection with the Gospel of Matthew, concerning
the Mission of the Hebrews and of the coming forth of
Christ Jesus from among this people. For, helped by
our study of the Gospels, clarity must gradually come
to us concerning the way the different streams of
spiritual life united, so that the great Christian stream
might later co-operate in common with these, for the
further evolution of the earth. In a short course of
lectures like this it is only possible to show in merest
outline what part fell to the share of the Hebrew people
in the general evolution of mankind. But the Gospel
of Matthew cannot be understood unless we consider
to some extent at least certain other features of this
people. To do so we must bring clearly before our souls
in what their mission really consisted. We have seen
how this differed from the missions of other Christian
peoples; these were still connected with what we may
call the experiences of the old form of clairvoyance.
Such experiences were found among all ancient peoples,
and might at the same time be called ancient Wisdom.

Were we to describe this in an entirely external way
we would say : in ancient Atlantis men in general could
still see into the spiritual world. Granted that the
experiences of Initiates were of a higher order, yet

every one had some idea of the spiritual world; while in
certain transitional states of consciousness the men of
that day could still see into spiritual realms. These
faculties were, however, to be replaced by that which at
the present time is man's principal faculty—the activity
of the mind, the acquiring of understanding of the outer
world by means of the physical senses, in short, by life
in the physical world. Very slowly and gradually this
was acquired in the long course of pre-Christian development. So that we can say : in the ancient Indian people
a rich residue of the old clairvoyance still remained.
What was taught by the Holy Rishis was an inheritance
from ancient times; it was a primeval wisdom. Even in
the second cultural epoch—the ancient Persian—what
was known and taught by the followers of Zarathustra
was founded on this inheritance from the old clairvoyance. In a similar way Chaldean astronomy was
permeated by ancient wisdom, as was also that of Egypt.
A science that calculated in accordance with the post-
Atlantean faculties of man would not have been understood by either Egyptian or Chaldean. A science which
expressed itself in the form of ideas and conceptions,
a science of a physical kind did not then exist. There
was no such type of thought as is prevalent to-day.

It is necessary that we should grasp the difference
between a true seer of our time and one of ancient
Chaldea or Egypt. The difference is very great. With
anyone who really attains to "seer-hood" in accordance
with the natural course of progress of our day, the case
is as follows : he receives what can be called manifesta-

tions from the spiritual world; he receives presentations, experiences, from the spiritual world in such a way that he has to permeate these experiences with his ordinary earthly thinking, with the logical understanding he has gained here in earthly existence. The experiences of a seer of modern times can in no way be understood if these have not come to a soul already trained, in an ordered way, in logical and clear thought. Otherwise these present-day revelations remain incomprehensible; they demand that the soul should approach them with logical thought. Anyone who has such experiences without the will to logical thinking, without the will to self-denying understanding, training, and development of his earthly powers, attains to a visionary clairvoyance that can in no way be understood, a clairvoyance that remains incomprehensible and therefore misleading. Only a soul with a will sufficiently strong to learn in an intelligent way can attain to the present-day inspirations of seer-hood. Therefore in a spiritual movement like ours, the greatest value is laid on the fact that the training of the power of vision should be no one-sided development, that manifestations from the spiritual world should be announced in no one-sided way, but that they must be worked for, that the soul must bring something to meet these revelations and experiences. Logical endeavour has also to be employed if it is desired to develop the power of inner vision; these two cannot be separated in our days. It was quite otherwise with the seer of Egypt or Chaldea. He received along with his inspirations, which followed a quite different path, the laws of logic. He had, therefore, no special need to study logic. When he had gone through a spiritual training the complete law was imparted to him along with his inspirations. The organism of the present day no longer serves for this; man has evolved past this stage, for evolution is ever progressing.

When this difference is kept clearly before us, it becomes quite comprehensible that relics of ancient clairvoyance were constantly found in pre-Christian times, with the single exception of the ancient Hebrew people. This people was destined to evolve a human organ capable of comprehending the outer physical world in accordance with measure, number, etc., and so gradually to rise from the physical world to a knowledge of what is spiritual as contained in the image of Jahve or Jehova.

The essential fact was, that in Abraham a man was specially chosen whose brain was so constructed that he could become the progenitor of a whole race, and could pass on his peculiar faculty to his descendants. They were not only to receive revelations that arose within their inner being, but they were also to regard as a gift that which came to them from outside.

Everything this people received from Abraham came to them in the first place not from within themselves, but as a revelation from outside. Through this, something of extraordinary importance was imparted to them which distinguished the whole framework of this people from other races of antiquity—that distinguished it radically.

You can understand that the old faculties, the old inheritances were not lost all at once; that even among this people relics of former conditions continued. This is seen in Joseph, who had much in common with other peoples. He was therefore suited to form a link between the old Hebrews and the Egyptians, who were a people entirely within the spiritual influence of pre-Christian races.

Why should a people be so specially prepared? Why should a people be chosen and set apart from the rest of pre-Christian spiritual life, and why were these people endowed with special qualities?

This had to be, so that it might be possible to prepare mankind for the great moment when Christ Jesus was to come to earth. At this time ancient clairvoyance and blood relationship had fulfilled their purpose and something new was to come to pass for humanity: namely, the full use of the ego. Through the thorough admixture of blood, something that had great importance in the past, lost its meaning, and was replaced by the full employment of the ego. Thus the actual human kingdom or the "Kingdom of Heaven," was now added to the other kingdoms.

Humanity in general is not, however, entirely fitted to recognise new things when they appear. Events occurring in the Spirit are not recognised at once as such. People constantly speak lightly of some prophet who is to come in the future : this was common in pre-Christian as in post-Christian times. In the twelfth and thirteenth centuries there was an earnest search for prophets. In different places men arose who declared that in the near future Christ would come again; they even indicated the place where this was to occur. Such appearances even took place occasionally at other times. People spoke of this or that individual as an incarnation of a new Christ. Naturally it is unnecessary to waste words on such prophecies, for on the face of them their flaws are clearly discernible. Such prophecies have one constant defect: they speak prophetically of something that is to happen, but they neglect to prepare men so that they can recognise the event when it does come—to bring souls to such a state of perception that they are really able to understand the coming event. Men to whom such declarations are made have to experience something similar to the school teacher of whom Hebbel reports in his notes: he says this teacher beat a pupil because he could not understand Plato; Hebbel adds jokingly that this pupil might himself be a reincarnation of Plato! It is exactly the same with those who constantly speak of a Christ who is to reappear. It might well happen that they would be ill-prepared for the event if He did come: such people would take the Christ for something very different from what He really is. Preparation had, however, now to be made for this, and understanding of it is necessary to an understanding of the Gospel of Matthew, so that there may be at least a few capable of comprehending the Event of Christ. If we are to describe the Event from this side it consists in knowing that the Christ was He Who made it possible, from that time on, to receive not merely physical impressions from outside, but to receive the Spirit in this way also. For this a special class of men had to be prepared.

There have been in fact, all through ancient Hebrew history, certain people who were specially prepared that they might gain an understanding of the Event of Christ. There were but few of these among the ancient Hebrews, but we must study these men more closely if we are to understand the nature of the preparations made for the coming Christ, and how this people with the qualities they had inherited from Abraham, were rendered capable of understanding prophetically that the human ego was to be brought to them for their salvation (Heiland). The men, who were prepared to know, and recognise clairvoyantly what the Christ really stood for, were called Nazarenes. They perceived clairvoyantly what it was that had been prepared within the ancient Hebrew race so that Christ could be born from among them and be understood by them.

The Nazarenes were bound by strict rules in their inner life, these rules were laid down with due regard to their inner constitution, because of the clairvoyance they had developed, and because the age to which they belonged was quite different from ours. Though resembling them to some extent, these rules must be clearly distinguished from those according to which one attains the development of spiritual knowledge to-day. Much was of importance to the sect of Nazarenes which to-day is only of comparative importance, and much that is of great importance to-day was held by it to be only relatively so. Therefore no one should think that what led formerly to a man becoming a "knower" of Christ. clairvoyantly, leads in a modern sense to similar important and fruitful knowledge.

The first thing demanded of a Nazarene was complete abstinence from alcoholic drink of any kind: further, he was strictly forbidden to eat anything prepared with vinegar. Those who held very strictly to the instructions laid down were further obliged to avoid everything that came from the grape. Men held that with the grape the principle of plant-formation passed beyond a certain point, beyond the point where the sun-forces alone work upon them. They held that not only sun-forces were active in grapes, but something else was active in them which evolved inwardly, ripening every year as the sun-forces declined in strength, something which had power in autumn. Hence that which was connected with the grape only supplied a drink for those who did not wish to become clairvoyant in the higher sense, who wished merely to honour the God Dionysos, permitting their faculties to spring, as it were, from the earth. The Nazarene was further bound, so long as his training in Nazarene principles continued, never to come in contact with anything that died while in possession of an astral body—in short, anything of an animal nature. This he had to avoid. He had to be a vegetarian in the strictest sense of the word; and so in some circles the strictest Nazarenes chose for nourishment the locust bean; these beans were a common form of food for those who strove towards a Nazarene training. They also fed on honey from wild bees, not the culti-

vated bees, and from other honey-storing insects. Such
means of supporting life were chosen later by John the
Baptist, of whom we are told that he fed on locusts and
wild honey. This statement in the Gospels is misleading; the locusts there mentioned are not insects,
creatures which are not found in the desert, but the
locust bean (Johannisbrot). I have pointed out similar
mistakes on other occasions. Among the Nazarenes it
was held necessary, as a preparation for clairvoyance
and as long as this preparation lasted, not to cut the
hair; all these customs were intimately connected with the
whole evolution of mankind. Even this one, of permitting
the hair to grow long, has to be viewed in connection
with the whole evolution of man; everything in man
that is living can only be understood when comprehended from the side of the spirit. Strange as it may
sound, we have to see in our hair a relic of certain out-
pourings by which the force of the Sun was formerly
conveyed to man. Formerly what the sun forces poured
into man was something living. Therefore, where
people still have a consciousness of deeper things, we
often find, for instance, in ancient carvings of lions,
that the sculptor does not simply represent lions with
their manes as we see them to-day. People in whom
traditions of ancient knowledge were still strong, represented the lion in such a way that one receives the
impression that the mane of the lion is stuck into his
body as it were from outside; they are like rays from the
sun that have streamed into him and been hardened into
hair. Thus people said: it was perhaps still possible in

olden times to receive forces into one by allowing the hair to grow long, especially if it were strong and healthy. But by the time of the Nazarenes the Hebrews saw hardly anything more in it than a symbol.

In certain connections human progress really consisted in man allowing that which lives spiritually behind the sun to stream into him. In the advance made from the old gift of clairvoyance to that of the power to combine thoughts concerning the surrounding world, it was ordained that he should appear as a being ever less endowed with hair. We must picture the men of Atlantis and of early post-Atlantean times as having a strong growth of hair, a sign that the rays of spiritual light still shone powerfully upon them. A choice was made, as we are told in the Bible, between the smooth-skinned Jacob and the hairy Esau, in whom we have to see a man descended from Abraham, but who retained within him the last relic of an ancient evolution which found expression in his hairy development. Men, possessed of qualities such as he had evolved in the world, are represented by Jacob, who possessed the gift of cleverness in all its varied degrees. Esau was pushed aside by him. In Esau another branch of the main line was cut off. From him sprang the Edomites in whom old inherited qualities still continued. All these things are beautifully and exactly expressed in the Bible. A consciousness of what spiritual life is had to arise once more in mankind, and it arose in a new manner among the Nazarenes, as was shown in their wearing their hair long during their period of training. Long ago the relationship of hair to the light of the Spirit is revealed by the fact that light and hair, with the exception of a sign to which we attach little importance, are expressed by the same word. The ancient Hebrew language points ever to the profoundest secrets of humanity, and must therefore be regarded as a powerful revealer of wisdom. This was at the basis of the practice among the Nazarenes of allowing their hair to grow long, and need no longer be regarded as a matter of much importance.

During their period of training the Nazarenes had to arrive at a quite clearly defined clairvoyant experience; this was to give them an idea of how near humanity was to the time of the coming of Christ. The last great Nazarene of the time of Christ was John the Baptist. He had not only experienced the highest results of Nazarene training in himself, but could enable others whom he desired to bring to true manhood, to experience them also. The crown of this training was the " Baptism of John." We have to try to understand how great its value was in the course of evolution. What was this baptism and to what did it lead? It consisted in the first place in a man being dipped under water, by means of which his etheric body was somewhat loosened from the physical body, whereas otherwise it is closely united with it. You know that in drowning, as a result of the loosening of his etheric body, a man sees in a flash a picture of his whole life. In the baptism by John this also took place; a man beheld the events of his whole life, things that otherwise he had quite forgotten. He also saw what he was at that particular moment. The physical body is evolved by its constructor the etheric body; this member of the human being, although it forms the physical body, can only be perceived when it is loosened from it: this happened at the baptism by John.

If anyone had experienced this kind of baptism 3000 years before our era he would have known that the highest spirituality that could be imparted to men had to come to him as an ancient inheritance (for what came to man from the spiritual worlds in olden times was really still an inheritance); it was like a picture in the etheric body, and it formed the physical body. At this form of baptism it was especially revealed to those who were evolved beyond normal humanity, how all their knowledge rested on ancient inspiration; such men were represented, according to the vision of the etheric soul-nature, in the form of Serpents; and those who had experienced (the vision) were called the "Children of the Serpent," because they had perceived how deeply Luciferic Beings had entered into mankind. That which formed the physical body was a creation of the Serpent.

But now, at a baptism that took place not 3000 years before John the Baptist, but in his day, something quite different was apparent, namely, that among those who were baptised there were already some who showed in their nature that human evolution had advanced, and that an Ego, which had been fructified from the world around, possessed this great power. An entirely different picture was then revealed from that seen formerly at a baptism in the sense of John : men no longer saw the creative force of the etheric body in the likeness (Bild) of the Serpent, but in the likeness of the *Lamb*. This etheric body was no longer permeated from within with that which came from Luciferic forces, but it was entirely given over to the spiritual world which, because of the great things that had come to pass in the outer world, now illumined the souls of men. This vision of the lamb was experienced at the baptism of John by those who were able really to understand what this baptism meant at that time. These were they also who could say of themselves : man must be changed, he must become an entirely new being. The few who experienced this at the baptism by John could say : a mighty event has taken place, man has become different; the Ego has now gained the mastery on earth !

The people who were baptised by John had been prepared to understand the signs of the times, and they knew that this great event had come to pass.

Such was ever the mission of the Nazarenes. By baptism they were brought to the knowledge of the imminence of the Advent of Christ. They realised it through the loosening of their etheric bodies during baptism. John the Baptist had to declare that the time had now arrived when the ego could enter into human nature. He was recognised by this as he who fulfilled the times that had gone before; he was able to gather round him a company to whom he could show that through the change that had taken place in the ego, the Christ-Principle could now enter into man. John the Baptist had developed the Nazarene practice and teaching to its highest point, so that from being prophecy it had reached fulfilment. He formed around him a community able to understand the approaching Christ Event. Only in this sense can the words that the Baptist spoke be understood. Words spoken by him have to be accepted in all their infinite depth, and it is no longer fitting that a humanity desirous of occupying itself with such matters to-day, should see in John the Baptist nothing more than a shouting fanatic who insulted the Pharisees, calling them a generation of vipers, and saying to them: "Think not to say to yourselves we have Abraham for our Father, for God is able of these stones to raise up children unto Abraham."

John the Baptist would truly have been a strange kind of scold if he had not rejoiced that Pharisees and Sadducees came to him to be baptised. Yet he finds fault with them as soon as they come. Why does he do so? When these things are understood from their inner side, we see very soon that fanatical abuse alone does not lie behind these words, but that they really have a profound significance, a very deep meaning. But this meaning can only be understood when we realise a special tendency in the ancient Hebrew people.

From what has already been said, you can gather that Abraham was a man specially chosen, a man who had been so constituted or organised that at the right moment the Christ could be born from among his descendants. In order that this could come to pass the original attribute possessed by him had to be developed. We must realise that it was necessary to the development of this attribute that certain things had ever to be cast off. We have already seen how Joseph was cast off, but before that many others had also been cast off; for instance, Esau, the progenitor of the Edomites, because in him an ancient inheritance had remained from former times. Only that quality had to be preserved which was endowed with the distinguishing attribute of Abraham. This is expressed in a wonderful way, through the fact that Abraham had two sons, Isaac, the son of Sarah, on the one hand, and Ishmael. The ancient Hebrew people descended from Isaac. Abraham possessed, however, other qualities. If these had been handed down through the generations, the right bent would not have been given to the race. Hence these others had to be rigorously confined within another line of descendants, in that of Ishmael, the son of Hagar, the Egyptian serving maid. Thus two lines of descent proceeded from Abraham, one through Isaac, the other through the banished Ishmael; this line had in it the blood of an Egyptian woman and could not contain qualities appropriate to the mission of the Hebrew race.

Something very extraordinary now came to pass!

The Hebrews had to hand down in the line of descent the qualities right and fitting for them, and the ancient wisdom—an older inheritance—had to be imparted to them from outside; they had to go to Egypt so that they might receive what could be imparted to them there.

Moses was able to impart this ancient wisdom to the Hebrews because he was an Egyptian Initiate. He certainly could not have done so if he had possessed this only in the Egyptian form. It would be a mistake to think that Egyptian wisdom could be simply grafted on to that which flowed down from Abraham. This could never have been supported within the culture of the Hebrews; it would have produced a cultural deformity. Moses added to his Egyptian initiation something quite different. Therefore what he had acquired through this initiation could not be passed on so simply by him to the Israelites. He first imparted something to them after he had received the revelation on Sinai, that is, when he was outside Egypt. What was the revelation he received on Sinai? What did Moses receive there, and what did he give to this people? He gave them something well fitted to be engrafted on this race, because it was connected with it in a very special way. At one time the descendants of Ishmael had wandered from their native country and settled in the regions through which Moses now travelled with his people. Those qualities which had passed to the Ishmaelites by way of Hagar, and which, though certainly connected with Abraham, yet retained along with the special ones possessed by him many ancient inheritances, were found by Moses among the Ishmaelites, who had Initiates of their own. Because of the revelations received by this branch of the race, it was possible for Moses to make the revelations of Sinai comprehensible to the Israelites. There is an ancient Hebrew legend which tells: in Ishmael an off-shoot from the root of Abraham was pushed out towards Arabia. This means into the desert. That which developed in this branch was equally a part of the teaching of Moses. The ancient Hebrews received back through Moses, as the teaching of Sinai, what they had cast out of their blood: this came back to them again from outside.

Here once more we see the strange mission of the ancient Hebrew race; everything had to be imparted to it in such a way that it was received back again later, as a gift. As a gift from outside, Abraham had the whole Hebrew people restored to him in Isaac; Moses and his people received again from the descendants of Ishmael that which they had discarded. During its period of separation this people was not only to develop its own organisation, but was to receive back again as a gift from their God, that which they had cast from them. One has really to read the Bible very carefully, if one is to estimate aright the full importance of the words it contains. Such things run, as a characteristic feature, all through the history of the Hebrew people. Something sprang from the descendants of Hagar that was connected with the "Law-giving" of Moses, while the blood, which represented the peculiar faculty of the Israelites, sprang (abstammt) from Sarah.

Agar or Hagar has the same meaning as Sinai in the Hebrew tongue. It means the pinnacle or the Hill of Stones. One can also say: Moses received his

revelation of the law from the great stone, which stone
is an external representation of Hagar. What the
Jewish people received as "the Law" did not originate
from the best faculties of Abraham, but from Hagar,
from Sinai. So that those who were merely followers
of the law as given to Moses on Sinai—the Pharisees
and Sadducees—were exposed to the danger of remaining fixed in their development. These are they who,
at the baptism by John, did not wish to see the *Lamb*,
but the Serpent. Thus what otherwise seemed merely
scolding on the part of the Baptist, is changed into a
beautiful warning to the Pharisees and Sadducees,
when he cried to them : Ye who are the followers of the
Serpent, take care ye really see the right thing in
baptism, namely, not the Serpent, but the Lamb. And
he said further to them that they should not build on
the fact that they had Abraham for their father, for
this had become merely an expression with them, they
swore by that which came from the Stone Sinai, but this
had ceased to mean anything to them. Something like
a *new-born ego* was now to draw nigh from out the
world : "This ego I make known to you," declared
John the Baptist. "I make known unto you, how out
of Judaism will develop *that* which really has come down
through the generations, which can no longer be sworn
to on the single stone of Sinai, but on all that
surrounds us on every hand. Because of this, Children
of God will appear who will be able to see the Spirit
behind the world of the senses. Out of these stones the
Word of God can call forth children for Abraham !

You do not in the least understand the expression :
We have Abraham for our Father."

These words first acquire their full meaning from
what has been said here. Such things are not
only derived from the Akashic Chronicle; they are
stated in the Bible. Compare this with what Paul said
concerning them in his letter to the Galatians (Gal. iv.,
24-25). What I have just said is confirmed by the
Apostle Paul. He also says that Hagar or Agar is the
same word as Sinai, that what was given on Sinai was
a Testament, beyond which those men will evolve who,
because they have developed throughout the generations the special attribute of Abraham, will be able to
understand what has come into the world through Christ
Jesus. At the same time, reference is made to a saying
that must be understood in the future. It is a pity that
in an age when man has trained his intelligence appar-
ently so highly, he has yet pondered over things so
little ! For instance, over the expression : Repent !
According to its meaning it should be translated somewhat as follows : Bring about a change in your minds !

In many different places we are told that John
baptised to repentance, that is, to a change of mind
through water. As the baptised person came from the
water, his mind was to be changed, he was no longer to
look back to ancient traditions, but to look forward to
that which was to take possession of his free ego, the
ego that had become free through Christ Jesus. The
mind was to be turned from the direction of the old gods
into that of the new Spiritual Beings, or gods. In this

way, a change of mind was the aim of the baptism of
John. John baptised with water in order to call forth
in individuals the power to recognise that the Kingdom
of Heaven is at hand, and that through it they might
understand Who Christ Jesus is.

With this something more is added to what we had
previously learnt concerning the mission of the ancient
Hebrew people. It all leads to a gradual better understanding of the Christ. Most wonderfully all the
different parts of this mission are assembled. We have
seen how in Abraham was organised that which was to
develop further throughout the generations. In order
that this could come to pass much had to be rejected, so
that the fitting qualities could continue to evolve, by
inheritance, in the blood of the race. These qualities
could only be acquired by man from outside; but the
purpose, for which this people was chosen and set apart
from the times of Abraham, was concentrated within
one Being, even Jesus.

The Jews required something to which they could
cling as a teaching; this had always to come to them
from outside, and in fact it came to them from what they
had themselves rejected.

That which came to them through Ishmael was not
to remain in their blood, it was only to exist in their
cognition. Hence the Hebrews received this again in
the Law-giving on Sinai. This law had fulfilled its
purpose when the time had come in which men no longer
required what had come from the Stone, but when they
had received that which was to come to them from out

the whole world. Thus preparation was slowly made
for the time when Sons of God—that is, men—could
arise from stones; when behind all stones, yea, behind
the whole earth, the spiritual world would reveal itself.

All these things are but gradations that may help
to an understanding of the mission of the Hebrew
people. It is only when this mission is fully understood that the mighty form of Christ Jesus as presented
to us in the Gospel of Matthew, can be understood.

Lightning Source UK Ltd.
Milton Keynes UK
UKHW022049140223
417031UK00021B/279

9 781258 112738